SECRET BLIND ITEMS & LUXURY COCKTAILS:

From A Former Bartender At "The Most Opulent" Hotel & Resort Brand

LIANA BONNANI

Secret Blind Items & Luxury Cocktails: From A Former Bartender At "The Most Opulent" Hotel & Resort Brand

Published by FOWGID Publishing 2024

ISBN Ebook: 979-8-9909930-7-5;
ISBN Paperback: 979-8-9909930-8-2

CONTENTS

Introduction 07
Essential Supplies 08

Blind Item No. 1 - The Hip Hop Dasher
Cocktail - Lemondrop Martini (vodka base)................................ 10

Blind Item No. 2 - The Kissing Bandit
Cocktail - Notoriously Naked (mezcal base)............................13

Blind Item No. 3 - The Leader of the Pack
Cocktail - The Don (tequila based) 15

Blind Item No. 4 - The Queen of Hugs
Cocktail - Spiced Sangria (red wine and whiskey base)..............18

Blind Item No. 5 - The Coolest Frontman
Cocktail - Classic Dry Blue Cheese Martini (can be vodka or gin based) 20

Blind Item No. 6 - The Expletive-Laden Actor
Cocktail - Sidecar Holiday (cognac base) 22

Blind Item No. 7 - The Generous Actor
Cocktail - Vesper Martini (vodka *and* gin base)...........................25

Blind Item No. 8 - The Energized Singer
Cocktail - Espresso Martini (vodka base)............................28

Blind Item No. 9 - The Big Sister
Cocktail - Paris 75 (cognac and champagne base)....................31

Blind Item No. 10 - The Rustic Fellows
Cocktail - EFFEN Black Cherry Orange Bomb (vodka base)......34

Blind Item No. 11 - The Dine and Dash Heroes
Cocktail - Margot Mint Julep (bourbon base)............................36

Blind Item No. 12 - The Movie Producer/Philanthropist
Cocktail - Paloma (tequila base) 39

Blind Item No. 13 - Mr. Keep It Fresh
Cocktail - Classic Mojito Mejor (rum base)..................................42

Blind Item No. 14 - The Elder Statesman
Cocktail - Negroni Casoni (gin base) 44

Blind Item No. 15 - The Maestro
Cocktail - Canadian Old Fashioned (bourbon base)...................46

Blind Item No. 16 - The Stoic Actor
Cocktail - Vanderbilt Strong (bourbon base)...............................48

Blind Item No. 17 - The 90's Ladies Who Lunch
Cocktail - The Marseille (gin base) 50

Blind Item No. 18 - The G.O.A.T.
Cocktail - Empire Sour (whiskey base)..52

Blind Item No. 19 - The Mentalist
Cocktail - Daiquiri La Miel (rum base) 54

Blind Item No. 20 - The Questionable Doc
Cocktail - Lychee Martini (vodka base) 56

Blind Item No. 21 - The Sour Diva
Cocktail - The Revel (cognac/red wine base)...............................58

Blind Item No. 22 - The Flasher
Cocktail - Coco Loco Martini (rum and vodka base)...................61

Blind Item No. 23 - The Supporting Characters
Cocktail - Limoncello Delight (Limoncello/prosecco base) 64

INTRODUCTION

As a former bartender at an outpost of one of those very tony, very high end "The Most Opulent" Hotel & Resorts, and as an employee who has traveled to many worldwide locations of the brand for vacation, I have experienced a plethora of eye-popping and hilarious moments, paired with the best drinks life has to offer.

The clientele of "The Most Opulent" fall into three categories. You have your uber-wealthy, millionaire and billionaire types that walk amongst us peasants looking like normal people. You have your celebrities, A-List, to D-List, who may or may not be "wealthy", but are heavy on charisma and attitude. And finally you have your looky-loos, who know that if they sit at the bar or at your cocktail table drinking their $6 soda for long enough, they will see someone famous. And to be fair, they are not wrong.

So, mix yourself an opulent and luxurious cocktail. Plop down on your couch and be entertained by the experiences of our team as we rolled out the ultimate in quality drinking experiences. There is almost no request we could deny our discerning guests. We truly labored under a standard of the customer being in command of their own experience. We were there to make it happen!

Essential Supplies

Regarding your cocktail supplies, you do not need to have every bottle and mixer that we suggest in this book. Honestly, most people don't keep a fully stocked bar at home. They purchase bottles and supplies for occasions, and what they happen to enjoy the most. You can also substitute for any other brand of the recipe prescribed liquor you prefer. There are a few items you will want to have on hand however, for almost every recipe, and cocktail creation in general.

We will list those items here for you:

- Cocktail Shaker/Strainer
- Jigger to measure ounces
- Knife
- Wine Opener
- Wine Glass
- Martini Glass
- Highball Glass
- Rocks Glass
- Coupe Glass
- Champagne Flute
- Lemons
- Limes
- Oranges
- Blue Cheese Stuffed Olives
- Sparkling Water
- Tonic Water
- Simple Syrup - (recipe immediately below)
- Plenty of fresh ice

Elements of Simple Syrup

- 1 cup white sugar
- 1 cup water

Preparation of Simple Syrup

- Bring water and sugar to a boil in a saucepan.
- Stir sugar until dissolved.
- Let the mixture cool.
- Store in an airtight container for up to 1 month.

BLIND ITEM NO. 1 - **THE HIP HOP DASHER**

Cocktail - Lemondrop Martini (vodka base)

This hip-hop mogul and label head had a swagger that turned heads and instilled fear in hearts everywhere he went. He would saunter into "The Most Opulent" lounge to meet his artists, and other colorful characters while running up large tabs on his table. He demanded only the finest — top-shelf liquors, imported cigars, and exclusive VIP treatment. His favorite thing to do was to vanish from the lounge without paying because he knew that the staff was not going to force the issue with him. He would sometimes come back later to pay his bill if he remembered. Or the managers *might* present him with a previous bill the next time he came in, but this was rare. There were some servers he liked more than others and he would always request for them to wait on him, even if he was not sitting in that server's section of tables. One bright afternoon, he came in with one of his girlfriends, ordered a delectable lunch, and per usual, walked out without paying. This time however, the bar

  Secret Blind Items & Luxury Cocktails

manager forced his server to go out on the front drive and knock on the tinted window of his SUV to ask for payment in front of everyone. This server was knocking on the window of his Range Rover, voice and knees shaking, asking him if he "could possibly" pay the check, to which he laughed and replied that he would come back and pay after he dropped his girlfriend back at home. To his credit, that time he did return to pay the check, probably more for the sake of that server than anything else. Classic move for someone used to making headlines.

Hip-Hop mogul didn't really drink much. But some of his girlfriends were partial to our famous **Lemondrop Martini** which we present here.

Lemondrop Martini

Elements

- 2 oz Belvedere Vodka or your favorite vodka
- ½ oz Cointreau
- ½ oz of simple syrup
- 1 oz freshly squeezed lemon juice
- fine sugar to garnish glass

Preparation

1. The Lemondrop Martini is best with a sugar rimmed glass so you will want to prepare your glass first.
2. On a small plate spread out your fine sugar.
3. Take a lemon wedge and run it around the rim of your glass until the juice is visible.
4. Dip the rim of your glass into the sugar, then place your glass into the freezer for 15 minutes.
5. Next fill your cocktail shaker with ice, then add your vodka, lemon juice, Cointreau, and simple syrup.
6. Shake until you get a strong freeze on your shaker.
7. Strain into your prepared glass. Add lemon wedge, twist or wheel as garnish.

Sip and dream of sunny days!

BLIND ITEM NO. 2 - THE KISSING BANDIT

Cocktail - Notoriously Naked (mezcal base)

This rugged and hard scrabble actor turned boxer, turned actor again, was greatly celebrated upon his starring return to film, which won him several awards. During winter awards season on the night of his big "golden" win, he came into "The Most Opulent" lounge after an awards show with friends to celebrate. He was so ecstatic to have won that he grabbed one of the cocktail servers who had congratulated him and kissed her squarely on the lips, much to her shock and chagrin. His celebrity friends who were along for the ride grabbed him and told him to calm down.

A fantastic and frisky drink for awards show celebrating is the **Notoriously Naked!**

Notoriously Naked

Elements

- ○ 1 oz Mezcal Vago Elote or your favorite mezcal
- ○ 1 oz Aperol
- ○ 1 oz Yellow Chartreuse liqueur
- ○ 1 oz lime juice
- ○ orange twist or lime wedge for garnish if desired

Preparation

1. Prepare your glass first. This is best served up, in a chilled coupe glass. Pop yours into the freezer for 10 minutes.
2. Fill your cocktail shaker with ice.
3. Pour in your mezcal, Aperol, Yellow Chartreuse and lime juice.
4. Shake vigorously until you get a good freeze on the shaker.
5. Pour into your chilled glass.
6. Garnish with an orange twist or lime wedge if desired.

BLIND ITEM NO. 3 - **THE LEADER OF THE PACK**

Cocktail - The Don (tequila based)

Spotted: This ever dapper, leader of the pack Hollywood actor and filmmaker was seen seated at the "number 1 display table" in the front room of "The Most Opulent" lounge, immediately after breaking up with his sultry Vegas cocktail waitress girlfriend. Despite the split, this A-lister was all smiles and charm, radiating good spirits and keeping the mood light with what looked to be his agents and other film executives. He was very kind to our staff, and cut a dashing figure in his navy sweater looking every bit the new *available* bachelor. Was he on the prowl again? We don't know, as he didn't hit on any of our "The Most Opulent" staff no matter how many pretty cocktail waitresses dropped snack refills and cocktail linens on his table. However, he certainly seemed quite happy to be *freely* out and about. Seems like he's already moved on and is ready to focus on the next big blockbuster.

This gentleman really fancies a wonderful tequila. Enter our famous, **The Don** margarita.

The Don

Elements

- 1 ½ oz Don Julio Reposado tequila or your favorite tequila of choice
- 1 oz fresh squeezed lime juice
- 1 oz Cointreau
- ½ oz agave nectar or simple syrup
- lime wheels or wedges for garnish
- salt or chili spice for a rimmed glass if desired

Preparation

1. Prepare your glass first if you will be having a garnished rim. Run a lime wedge around the rim of your glass. You can use a rocks glass or margarita glass, whichever you wish. Dip the rim into your salt or chili spice, whichever you prefer.
2. Pour all of your ingredients into a cocktail shaker.
3. Fill with ice and shake vigorously until you have a good freeze on the shaker.
4. Strain into your ice filled prepared glass.
5. Garnish with lime wedge or wheel.

Savor!

BLIND ITEM NO. 4 - **THE QUEEN OF HUGS**

Cocktail - Spiced Sangria (red wine and whiskey base)

This soulful singing diva who had an old school hit that propositioned lovers in French came sailing through "The Most Opulent" lounge one brilliant afternoon showering smiles, laughter and the wonderful scent of her perfume on everyone she passed by. There was one member of our staff who was a huge fan of this belle and greeted her with glee. In return, they received the biggest, warmest mama-style hug and have not stopped talking about it since, even years later! This diva loves a good red wine. Something akin to our juicy **Spiced Sangria**.

Spiced Sangria (serves 6)

Elements

- 1 bottle of spicy fruity wine, a shiraz or pinot noir will work
- 1 cup of Jack Daniels Tennessee Fire or your favorite spiced/cinnamon whiskey
- 1 cup apple cider
- ¼ cup orange juice
- 1 apple cut up
- ½ orange cut up
- ½ cup simple syrup to taste (optional)

Preparation

1. Stir your wine, whiskey, and apple cider together into a large pitcher or drink dispenser to mix.
2. Taste and decide if you would like to add in simple syrup.
3. Add the sliced apples and oranges and stir again.

Relish!

BLIND ITEM NO. 5 - **THE COOLEST FRONTMAN**

Cocktail - Classic Dry Blue Cheese Martini (can be vodka or gin based)

No one could command a room quite like this charismatic singer. This British musician and frontman for a wildly popular 80's New Wave band was generous enough to spontaneously get up and sing in the back room of the lounge on a night when our regular live house band was playing. How thrilling to hear his dulcet tones singing of love set free. Indeed this was an unforgettable memory for everyone lucky enough to witness his impromptu performance, guests and staff alike.

New Wave is now classic. We enjoy his singing with a classic **Dry Blue Cheese Dirty Martini!**

Classic Dry Blue Cheese Dirty Martini

Elements

- ½ oz Dolin Dry Vermouth or your favorite dry vermouth
- 3 oz Belvedere Vodka or Gin Mare Gin (whichever liquor you prefer)
- 1 oz of olive brine
- olives
- blue cheese (you can also purchase pre-stuffed cheese olives by the jar at any quality liquor store, but making your own is fun!)

Preparation

1. Prepare your glass first. Rinse your glass with the vermouth and chill it in the freezer for 15 minutes.
2. Hand stuff your olives with as much blue cheese as you can fit inside, then put them on a small skewer. Alternatively, you can skewer your pre-stuffed olives.
3. Fill your cocktail shaker with ice, then mix in your chosen liquor, olive brine and vermouth.
4. Shake until you feel a good freeze on the shaker.
5. Strain into your chilled glass and add your skewer of olives.

Sip!

BLIND ITEM NO. 6 - THE EXPLETIVE-LADEN ACTOR

Cocktail - Sidecar Holiday (cognac base)

The tall, handsome and fearsome actor who played a medical professional by day and was abruptly fired from his television series made "The Most Opulent" lounge his new clubhouse post-firing. This was a smart move considering no photos are allowed in the bar and his firing was the biggest story in Hollywood that season. He liked to begin his hang-outs in a very civilized manner, drinking hot tea and reading newspapers. But what started as a quiet retreat with afternoon tea soon turned into a nightly debauchery. As sunset began, he would move into drinking cognac at which time his personality would change completely. He could be found engaging the women guests on the outdoor patio, and making unwanted and risque comments to one of the

cocktail waitresses on our team. He told her he planned to have his way with her (in the coarsest way imaginable), even though no one was asking for this and he was married at the time.

Inspired by a cognac fueled search for a side piece is the **Sidecar Holiday** cognac cocktail.

Sidecar Holiday

Elements

- 1½ oz Remy Martin VSOP or your favorite VSOP cognac
- ½ oz yuzu liqueur
- ¾ oz fresh lemon juice
- ½ oz Monin Ginger Syrup
- orange wedge or rind for garnish
- granulated sugar for the glass rim

Preparation

1. Prepare your glass first. Using half a lemon wedge, coat the rim of coupe glass. Dip it into a plate of granulated sugar. Chill your coupe glass in the freezer for 10 minutes.
2. In your cocktail shaker filled with ice, combine cognac, syrup, liqueur and lemon juice.
3. Shake vigorously, until there is a nice freeze on the shaker.
4. Strain drink into rimmed coupe glass.
5. Garnish with orange peel or petite orange wedge, as you wish.

Partake!

BLIND ITEM NO. 7 - THE GENEROUS ACTOR

Cocktail - Vesper Martini (vodka *and* gin base)

This star of a now defunct prime time show that aired on one of the Big Four networks, played a federal agent all the hours of the day and night. He is also the son of a very famous television and film actor, so he walks in legacy. This actor made an unexpected appearance at "The Most Opulent" lounge one day, slipping into the outdoor patio and settling into one of the larger cabanas alone. He discreetly informed his cocktail server that he wished to keep things low-key, planning nothing more than an intimate birthday celebration with a few close friends. The cabana, designed to accommodate six, soon swelled to eight, and then fifteen guests. As the gathering outgrew its space, we made the executive decision to open the adjacent, closed restaurant, allowing him to have the entire area to himself. No prior reservation had been made for either space, but at "The Most Opulent" hotel, we are committed to crafting exceptional experiences, so we went above and beyond to

accommodate. To his credit, after all of his friends had eaten and drank their fill, this actor tipped the server half the cost of the bill. The dollar amount was enough to pay the server's rent for a month. Though the server kindly reminded him that gratuity had already been included, and his girlfriend gently advised against the additional tip, he was adamant. He explained that he knew firsthand the demands of waiting tables and appreciated the hard work involved. His remarkable generosity left a lasting impression, making it a day the server will undoubtedly remember for years to come.

In the spirit of agenting and spies, a lounge favorite was and still is the **Vesper Martini**.

Vesper Martini

Elements

- 3 oz Monkey 47 Gin or your favorite gin
- 1 oz Belvedere Vodka or your favorite vodka
- ¼ oz Lillet Blanc
- lemon peel for a twist garnish

Preparation

1. Pop your martini glass into the freezer for a quick chill while you prepare your cocktail.
2. In your beautiful cocktail shaker filled with ice, add your gin, vodka and Lillet Blanc.
3. Shake vigorously until you feel the freeze on your shaker.
4. Strain the mixture into your chilled martini glass.
5. Rub your lemon peel around the rim of the glass and then twist it into a spiral and drop it into the martini.

Serve!

BLIND ITEM NO. 8 - **THE ENERGIZED SINGER**

Cocktail - Espresso Martini (vodka base)

This prolific singer-songwriter and talent show judge has written some of the biggest and most celebrated songs of our time that probably had you dancing on the surface that is the opposite of the floor. He is one of the most personable people you will ever meet, perhaps as a result of his southern upbringing. He would come into "The Most Opulent" lounge, be greeted by friends and fans alike, and he would never turn anyone away. He took a special moment with one of our servers to encourage them to have fortitude in their career aspirations, and promised them that he believed they would not be waiting tables for very long. In the case of that server, he was quite right. They left the lounge within the year to move on to other creative pursuits.

This man has the energy of the energizer bunny, so our **Espresso Martini** is especially appropriate.

Espresso Martini

Elements

- 1 ½ oz Absolut Vanilla Vodka or your vanilla vodka of choice
- 1 oz Mr. Black Coffee Liqueur
- 1 oz espresso or cold brew concentrate
- ½ oz simple syrup or Bailey's Irish Cream (optional for extra sweetness)
- coffee beans for garnish (optional)

Preparation

1. Fill your cocktail shaker with ice, then mix in your chosen vodka, Mr. Black Coffee Liqueur, espresso and simple syrup/or Bailey's (if desired).
2. Shake vigorously until you feel a strong freeze on the shaker.
3. Strain into your glass.
4. Garnish with 3 coffee beans (if desired).

Drink and Buzz!

BLIND ITEM NO. 9 - **THE BIG SISTER**

Cocktail - Paris 75 (cognac and champagne base)

This older sister of a midwest singing family which produced *the* biggest pop icon of all time was a regular in "The Most Opulent" lounge. She loved chatting with all of the staff and sometimes inviting a friend with her to enjoy some white tablecloth dining. Now the bar is casual daytime dining, but the staff would go get table linens and special tableware to set up her bar table so that she could have her full five star, five diamond experience. To be fair, she was always very kind in her requests, and never demanding.

For this elegant lady, we will toast with a **Paris 75**.

Paris 75

Elements

- 1½ oz Rémy Martin 1738 Accord Royal or your favorite cognac
- ½ oz simple syrup
- ½ oz fresh lemon juice
- Perrier-Jouët Grand Brut Champagne or your favorite brut champagne
- lemon twist for garnish

Preparation

1. Combine Rémy Martin 1738 cognac or your favorite cognac, simple syrup and fresh lemon juice into your cocktail shaker and add ice.
2. Shake vigorously until the shaker has a nice freeze on it.
3. Strain into your champagne glass.
4. Top with Perrier-Jouët or your favorite champagne float.
5. Garnish with a lemon twist.

Salut!

BLIND ITEM NO. 10 - **THE RUSTIC FELLOWS**

Cocktail - EFFEN Black Cherry Orange Bomb (vodka base)

This monstrously successful country trio made the hotel their go-to retreat every time they were in town. Whenever they came down to the lounge, this band always claimed the largest table on the outdoor patio, enjoying drinks and cigars in true country fashion with a Hollywood twist. Needless to say, their generosity matched their success—they were excellent tippers. They had a favorite cocktail server who became close friends with the band and their families. Fortunate enough to earn their trust, she was often invited to their concerts and appearances, bringing along her own friends and family. They were truly some of the most fun and wonderful guests.

For a fun bunch like these cowboys, you have to have an **EFFEN Black Cherry Orange Bomb!**

EFFEN Black Cherry Orange Bomb

Elements

- 1 ½ oz EFFEN Black Cherry vodka
- 3 orange slices
- 8 blackberries (muddled fruit together will yield about 1 oz of juice)
- ½ oz simple syrup
- 1 oz Pellegrino or club soda

Preparation

1. In a mixing glass, muddle the fruit together.
2. Use a fork to remove all of your orange slices.
3. Add your simple syrup, vodka and fresh ice and shake vigorously.
4. Strain into a rocks glass filled with ice and add a 1 oz sparkling water float.
5. Garnish with a blackberry skewer.

To Your Health!

BLIND ITEM NO. 11 - **THE DINE AND DASH HEROES**

Cocktail - Margot Mint Julep (bourbon base)

Believe it or not, even in a hotel bar like the "The Most Opulent", there are those guests who delight in a game of dine and dash. They move the bill book to a different part of the table to make it look as though they've put payment inside of it. When the server has gone into the kitchen to get more snacks or cocktail linens, they take that opportunity to run out of one of the many exits. On one particular day when this occurred, the bar was also hosting two esteemed, award-winning actors who were celebrating the premiere of their football movie, inspired by true events. Upon hearing about the walkout, the tall, dark, and handsome lead actor approached his tall, blonde and handsome co-star and proposed that they settle the bill together. Their generous gesture not only covered the cost but also spared the cocktail server from receiving a write-up — a consequence of walkouts that could eventually lead to dismissal. In doing so, these actors truly helped preserve the server's job,

turning what could have been a disastrous situation into a memorable act of kindness.

These are southern gentlemen, hailing from New Orleans and Texas respectively, so in their honor we will sip our most elegant **Margot Mint Julep**.

Margot Mint Julep

Elements

- ○ 6 mint leaves
- ○ ¾ oz simple syrup
- ○ 1 oz Woodford Reserve Bourbon or your favorite bourbon
- ○ 3 oz Rivata Prosecco or your favorite dry prosecco

Preparation

1. In a mint julep cup or highball glass muddle mint leaves and simple syrup until the mint is dark green.
2. Do not over muddle the leaves as you will begin to release bitter flavors and you don't want that for this cocktail.
3. Pour in the bourbon, and stir to mix well.
4. Then add ice, and pour in the prosecco. Add your bitters last and swirl gently.
5. Garnish with a few mint leaves.

More Life!

 Secret Blind Items & Luxury Cocktails

BLIND ITEM NO. 12 - **THE MOVIE PRODUCER/ PHILANTHROPIST**

Cocktail - Paloma (tequila base)

This super wealthy-by-inheritance movie producer who lost all of his money and sadly is no longer with us, lived upstairs in the hotel for a long time, no doubt spending a big chunk of that inheritance from month to month. He was a friendly guest, always greeted the staff, tipped well and due to his generous nature, always had a bevy of friends and hangers-on when hosting in the bar lounge. He donated millions to political figures, causes of all persuasions, and no doubt while many opportunists viewed him as a limitless source of cash, our staff saw him simply as one of our more pleasant guests.

We pour out a little of our delicious and classic **Paloma** for this cool cat.

Paloma

Elements

- ○ 2 oz Casamigos Blanco Tequila or your favorite blanco tequila
- ○ 1 ½ oz fresh grapefruit juice
- ○ ¾ oz fresh lime juice
- ○ ½ ounce simple syrup
- ○ tiny pinch of salt
- ○ Pellegrino sparkling water or your favorite sparkling water
- ○ thin wedge of grapefruit, for garnish, and if desired a rosemary sprig

Preparation

1. Fill your cocktail shaker with ice. Pour in your tequila, grapefruit juice, lime juice, simple syrup, & the tiniest pinch of salt.
2. Shake well for 10 to 15 seconds, until there is a strong freeze on the shaker. Set aside.
3. Fill your highball glass with ice.

4. Pour in your liquid mix.
5. Pour a sparkling water float on top.
6. Garnish the drink with a thin wedge of grapefruit and if
    you like, the rosemary sprig as well.

Toast!

BLIND ITEM NO. 13 - MR. KEEP IT FRESH

Cocktail - Classic Mojito Mejor (rum base)

This music mogul and fashion entrepreneur was big on health and loved to drink freshly squeezed juices while visiting the bar. Known for his preference for youthful companions many decades his junior, he arrived at the lounge to rendezvous with one such young lady, who brought along her closest friends — both girls and boys. As she slipped away to join him privately, her friends were left at the table to while away the time, giggling, gossiping, and waiting endlessly for her return.

For a refreshing "healthy" adult beverage you can't do better than our **Mojito Mejor**.

Classic Mojito Mejor

Elements

- 5 mint leaves, plus a few more for garnish
- 2 oz Diplomatico Planas Rum or your favorite white rum
- 1 oz fresh lime juice
- ½ oz simple syrup
- Pellegrino, or your favorite sparkling water
- lime slices, for garnish

Preparation

1. In a highball glass muddle your mint leaves with the simple syrup and fresh lime juice.
2. Do not over muddle. If you break the leaves apart, the aromatics begin to make your drink bitter, and you do not want that.
3. Add your rum and gently stir all of the ingredients together.
4. Add your ice cubes until nearly full. Then pour a club soda float on top and garnish with some good looking mint leaves and lime wedges.

Toast to Life!

BLIND ITEM NO. 14 - **THE ELDER STATESMAN**

Cocktail - Negroni Casoni (gin base)

This esteemed veteran marquee actor, is well known for his iconic film about frolicking in the grass with a tragically fated Hollywood starlet. He frequently relished presiding over a table in the secluded back room of "The Most Opulent" lounge while hanging out with his buddies, attended to by his favorite, long-time server, whose lively conversation added to the charm of his visits. He always had a ready smile and a joke to keep the mood light.

This leading man actually doesn't drink alcohol, but if he did, we imagine he would enjoy the classic **Negroni Casoni.**

Negroni Casoni

Elements

- ¾ oz London Dry Gin by Tanqueray or your favorite gin
- ¾ oz Campari
- ¾ oz sweet vermouth Cinzano Rosso or your favorite sweet vermouth
- orange peel (for garnish)

Preparation

1. Combine all of your liquid ingredients with some ice in a shaker cup and stir gently, do not shake, until chilled, for about 30 seconds.
2. Strain into a rocks glass filled with ice.
3. Squeeze orange twist over the drink and slip it into the glass.

Tipple, tipple!

BLIND ITEM NO. 15 - **THE MAESTRO**

Cocktail - Canadian Old Fashioned (bourbon base)

This wonderful, legendary keyboardist and singer-songwriter would often come into "The Most Opulent" lounge with his manager plotting and planning big deals, performances and children's toy charity benefits over an elaborate afternoon tea service with a little side of brown liquor. His manager typically handled most of the ordering, serving as a buffer between him and overzealous fans, due to his physical challenges. Despite this, he was always gracious and kind to every server he encountered.

For this old school music maestro we offer our **Canadian Old Fashioned.**

Secret Blind Items & Luxury Cocktails

Canadian Old Fashioned

Elements

- 2 oz Michter's Bourbon or your favorite bourbon
- 3-4 dashes Angnostura Aromatic bitters
- ½ teaspoon maple syrup
- orange peel
- 1 maraschino cherry (optional)

Preparation

1. Cut your orange peel, from the side of your orange. Rub the pulp side of the peel on the rim of your rocks glass, then set peel to the side to use at the end.
2. Add the bourbon, bitters, and maple syrup to the glass and stir to mix well.
3. Add some ice then stir again.
4. Twist the orange peel over the glass to release the flavors and then slip the peel into the drink.
5. Add a maraschino cherry for garnish (if desired).

Enjoy every drop!

BLIND ITEM NO. 16 - **THE STOIC ACTOR**

Cocktail - Vanderbilt Strong (bourbon base)

In an earlier, perhaps less happy time of his life, this actor who starred on a mid-century period show came into the bar with his then girlfriend at the height of his new found fame. On this particular night, they came in after an awards show and he was in full tux regalia. They took their place at the "center display table" in front of the bar, where, true to his well-known tv character persona, he immediately focused on savoring whiskey with a dour expression on his face. Had it been his choice, the Maker's Mark would have flowed uninterrupted, but his girlfriend stepped in to curtail the indulgence.

For those who enjoy a fanciful whiskey drink, our **Vanderbilt Strong** is very refreshing.

Vanderbilt Strong

Elements

- 2 oz Makers Mark or your favorite bourbon
- 5 oz fresh lemon juice
- 3 muddled fresh strawberries
- ¾ oz honey
- lemon twist for garnish if desired

Preparation

1. Fill your cocktail shaker with ice and pour in all of the ingredients.
2. Shake vigorously until the shaker has a strong freeze on it.
3. Fill a rocks glass with ice.
4. Strain the cocktail into the glass.
5. Garnish with lemon twist if desired.

Indulge!

BLIND ITEM NO. 17 - THE 90'S LADIES WHO LUNCH

Cocktail - The Marseille (gin base)

These two beautiful actresses were spotted enjoying a "ladies who lunch" business meeting in the lounge. One of these actresses earlier in her career was the leading lady in a poetic, finger-snapping 90's romantic film with a cult following. The other was most recently on a famous sitcom as the gorgeous, hippy mama you love to love. Both of these ladies have increased their desirability, beauty and star power since the 90's by manifold amounts. According to our waitstaff they both were lovely to wait on and asked the servers about their own acting aspirations and projects, while offering plenty of suggestions and encouragement.

The perfect cocktail for a sunny afternoon business meeting is **The Marseille**, an elevated gin and tonic.

The Marseille

Elements

- 2 oz of Hendricks Gin or your favorite herbal gin
- 1 oz Elderflower liqueur
- ½ oz Pierre-Jouët Champagne or your favorite champagne
- ½ oz tonic water
- garnish with a lemon wedge and sage leaf or rosemary sprig (as preferred)

Preparation

1. In a glass filled with ice, pour in your gin, elderflower liqueur, tonic and champagne.
2. Stir gently.
3. Garnish with a lemon wedge and a sage leaf or the rosemary sprig as you wish.

Tipple!

BLIND ITEM NO. 18 - THE G.O.A.T.

Cocktail - Empire Sour (whiskey base)

This hip hop G.O.A.T. and master lyricist relocated to Los Angeles from New York in pursuit of new on-camera opportunities. He took up residence at "The Most Opulent" Hotel for a time before acquiring a family home. During his stay, he became a familiar and warmly regarded presence among our waitstaff, known for his  delightful and amiable demeanor. He certainly had his preferred servers, and in those days, a few of the ladies on our staff were particularly fond of wearing Hello Kitty diamond jewelry. With a twinkle in his eye, he would playfully inquire, "How is Kitty doing today?"— a question that never failed to elicit laughter from all within earshot.

In honor of this New York Legend, we raise a glass with the **Empire Sour.**

Empire Sour

Elements

- 2 oz Basil Hayden Dark Rye Whiskey or your favorite rye whiskey or bourbon
- 1 oz freshly squeezed lemon juice
- ½ to ¾ oz simple syrup to taste
- ½ to ¾ oz dry red wine, such as a cabernet
- lemon wheel for garnish if desired

Preparation

1. Fill your cocktail shaker with ice.
2. Add your whiskey, lemon juice and simple syrup.
3. Shake vigorously until your shaker takes on a nice freeze.
4. Strain the mixture into a rocks glass filled with ice.
5. Pour a red wine float on top by letting the wine flow slowly over the back of a spoon.
6. Garnish with lemon wheel if desired.

Partake!

BLIND ITEM NO. 19 - THE MENTALIST

Cocktail - Daiquiri La Miel (rum base)

This cerebral actor who enjoys discussing topics such as science, loved to come into "The Most Opulent" lounge and camp out on a six-top table alone, lingering over a single cup of tea for hours. For the avoidance of doubt, this was not afternoon tea service. This was just a normal cuppa. Despite the simplicity of ordering a cup of tea, he would keep his servers at the table for up to ten minutes, rambling about nothing in particular and unnecessarily putting the waitstaff in the weeds with the rest of their tables. All the while, he gradually eased into fully embodying his "tea-drinking character." If the server made any indication that they needed to move things along, he could become disgruntled and treat them very poorly.

For the waitstaff exasperated with these scenes, we sometimes turned to the comfort of a classic rum favorite, **Daiquiri La Miel**, *post-shift only*, of course.

Daiquiri La Miel

Elements

- 2 oz Diplomatico Planas or your favorite white rum
- 1 oz fresh lime juice
- ½ oz simple syrup
- lime wedge or twist for garnish
- For a fashionable old school look use a coupe glass

Preparation

1. Fill your cocktail shaker with ice, pour in your rum, lime juice and simple syrup and shake until you feel a good freeze on the shaker.
2. For an elegant look, strain into a coupe glass.
3. Garnish with lime wedge or twist.

Cheers!

BLIND ITEM NO. 20 - **THE QUESTIONABLE DOC**

Cocktail - Lychee Martini (vodka base)

This rather infamous plastic surgeon who has now lost his medical license on two separate occasions for issues relating to alcohol, DUI and malpractice, was at one time a semi-regular patron at "The Most Opulent" lounge. That is, up until his career famously and spectacularly blew up when a well known patient had a major problem post-surgery and many lawsuits were levied against him. In his after-work hours he was a big fan of our martinis. As a man who was as tall as the average NBA player, he was able to put away more than the average person.

Speaking of martinis, one of our more popular martinis, particularly at the Hawaiian property is the **Lychee Martini**.

Lychee Martini

Elements

- 1 ½ oz Belvedere Vodka or your favorite vodka
- 1 ½ oz St. Germain
- 1 oz lychee juice
- lychee fruit for garnish

Preparation

1. Pop your martini glass into the freezer to chill as you prepare your cocktail.
2. Pour your vodka, St. Germain and lychee juice into your cocktail shaker over ice.
3. Shake vigorously until you feel a good freeze on the shaker.
4. Strain into your favorite martini glass.
5. Garnish with a lychee fruit.

Cin Cin!

BLIND ITEM NO. 21 - THE SOUR DIVA

Cocktail - The Revel (cognac/red wine base)

This gorgeous Hollywood nepo-baby has been a romantic film lead for the last 25 years. She seems to be ageless. While she was a dating recording industry honcho responsible for breaking some of the biggest acts of 90's music, "The Most Opulent" lounge was one of their favorite places to hang out. Sadly, this actress had a sour attitude toward any female waitstaff working her table as though she was afraid that her boyfriend might be distracted by them. After a few drinks, she would lean back casually on her chair and openly glare at any woman who came by the table to clean up, take orders or deliver drinks. Her music honcho boyfriend often found himself apologizing to waitstaff for her antics. Her behavior provided our staff with no small amount of amusement.

So, for a woman who appreciates a good, devil-may-care drink and to hell with what may happen afterward, we offer **The Revel**.

The Revel

Elements

- 1 ¾ oz Hennessy VS Cognac or your favorite VS cognac
- ¾ oz of a claret wine (the more fruit forward the better)
- ½ oz fresh lemon juice
- ½ oz simple syrup
- pinch of freshly grated nutmeg (if desired), and a lemon wheel for garnish

Preparation

1. Chill a red wine glass for 10 minutes in your freezer.
2. In your cocktail shaker, combine the cognac, wine, lemon juice and simple syrup.
3. Then fill the shaker with ice and shake vigorously until you feel a nice freeze on it.

4. Strain into a chilled ice-filled red wine glass and garnish with the nutmeg (if desired).
5. Slip the lemon wheel into the beverage.

Raise Your Glass!

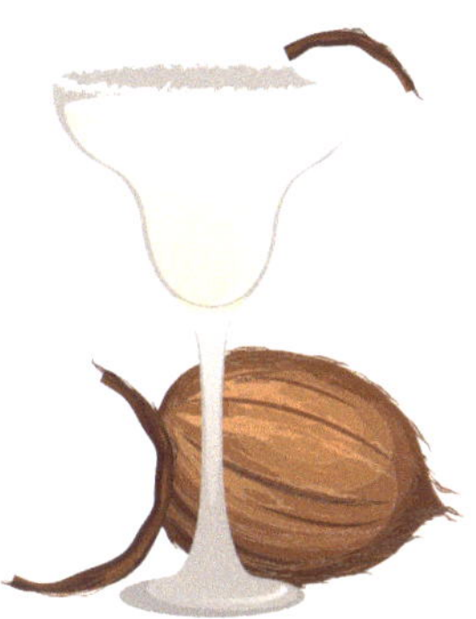

BLIND ITEM NO. 22 - THE FLASHER

Cocktail - Coco Loco Martini (rum and vodka base)

With the swagger of George Jefferson, this foul mouthed comedian and film actor known for his roles in a plethora of concert specials and slapstick comedies was 86'd (banned) from the lounge after getting drunk on the patio, speaking belligerently to the waitstaff, calling one particular server completely out of her name and as the cherry on the cake, dropping his pants to expose himself in front of a crowded and fully seated patio in broad daylight. Our staff was pretty happy to never have to wait on him again.

Let's cheers to 86'ing problematic people with a **Coco Loco Martini!**

Coco-Loco Martini

Elements

- 1 ½ oz Stoli Vanilla Vodka or your favorite vanilla vodka
- 1 oz of Koloa Kaua'i Coconut Rum or your favorite coconut rum
- ½ oz cream of coconut (sweetened) or if you want a thinner version use a canned coconut milk
- 1 splash fresh pineapple juice
- Coconut flakes for garnish (optional)
- Pineapple wedge, for garnish

Preparation

1. Chill a martini glass in your freezer for 10 minutes.
2. Muddle a few pineapple wedges for your "splash" of fresh pineapple juice. Reserve one small wedge for your glass garnish.
3. In your cocktail shaker, add your ice, then pour in the vodka, rum, cream of coconut, and pineapple juice. Shake vigorously until the shaker has a strong freeze on it.
4. Strain into your martini glass and add your pineapple garnish.
5. Sprinkle coconut flakes on top if desired.

Savor!

BLIND ITEM NO. 23 -
THE SUPPORTING CHARACTERS

Cocktail - Limoncello Delight (Limoncello/ prosecco base)

Not everyone who frequented the "The Most Opulent" Lounge was a celebrity.

There were many characters who held the lounge as their own personal clubhouse and offices.

There were Eastern European wiseguys who held nightly reserved tables.   They were big cash tippers that the wait staff would compete with each other to serve.

There were international ex-military characters who would show up every afternoon suited and booted just to read the paper and drink a glass of champagne.

There was royalty from the Middle East who would surreptitiously order alcohol and bacon through room service while asking for it to be put on a separate personal check that would not be seen by the royal administration staff at home.

There were everyday people who were willing to come in and spend half of their paycheck on a meal in a place where they could have the best chance to see the movers and shakers of the current day.

So many stories, so many drinks. Enjoy sipping on these special concoctions "The Most Opulent" Hotel uses to surprise and delight. In return, our guests surprised us with a few delightful moments of their own.

Ok, just one more drink....let's leave it on a bright note with a **Limoncello Delight**.

Limoncello Delight

Elements

- 2 oz Limoncello
- ½ oz ginger beer
- ¼ oz fresh lemon juice
- ½ oz Pellegrino or sparkling water
- 3 oz La Marca Prosecco or other sparkling wine
- fresh mint sprigs for garnish if desired
- lemon slices for garnish if desired

Preparation

1. Fill a large glass half full with ice.
2. Add your Limoncello, ginger beer, and lemon juice and stir gently.
3. Pour in your Pellegrino and prosecco and stir gently again.
4. If desired, add lemon wheels or slices, and mint for garnish.

Refresh!